Gallery Books
Editor: Peter Fallon

NIGHT TRAIN THROUGH
THE BRENNER

Harry Clifton

NIGHT TRAIN
THROUGH THE
BRENNER

Night Train through the Brenner
is first published
simultaneously in paperback
and in a clothbound edition
on 28 April 1994.

The Gallery Press
Loughcrew
Oldcastle
County Meath
Ireland

ISBN 1 85235 122 5 (*paperback*)
     1 85235 123 3 (*clothbound*)

The Gallery Press receives financial assistance from An Chomhairle
Ealaíon / The Arts C~~ouncil, Ireland~~

Contents

'*In our own city, we are exiles . . .*' page 11

Acknowledgements

Acknowledgements are due to the editors of *Force 10*, *Fortnight*, *The Honest Ulsterman*, *Ireland in Exile*, *The Irish Times*, *Krino*, *Poetry Ireland Review*, *Poetry Review*, *Rhinoceros*, *Stand*, *The Sunday Tribune* and *Verse* where some of these poems were published first.

A number of the poems in Part One featured in the pamphlet 'At the Grave of Silone: An Abruzzo Sequence' published by The Honest Ulsterman (1993).

for Deirdre

In our own city, we are exiles —
Strangers, through the closed windows
Of taxis, staring
At the selves we never became.

How they crowd there, the familiar faces
At the intersections! For them, too, the lights change
Like an illusion of freedom
As they disappear out of our lives.

Today Dublin, tomorrow Paris or Rome —
And the blur of cities
Is one City, simultaneous,
Eternal, from which we are exiled forever.

And I say to you, 'Let us make a home
In ourselves, in each other . . . ' as if streets
Or the statues of public men
Or all the doors we will never darken again

Are a vanished counterworld
To love, that throws us together
In the back seat of our own destiny
Where one dreams, and the other gives directions.

PART ONE

The Marriage Feast

Speeches, laughter, ripples of applause —
In the mind of God, in the blue Italian haze
Beyond Assisi, were they heard
Or forgotten, as if they had never occurred?
The rice in the streets? And the restaurant tablewine?
The waiters, Dino and Carlo, all attention?
As they feasted there, did it cross their minds —
In each according to his own apprehension —

What might have been? 'I heard the Sisters singing,'
She told herself, the mother of the bride,
'From the depths of Poor Clare convents, while I laid
My daughter's bridal trousseau on the bed,
And wondered again if it were mine to choose
The strife of wedlock, or that chaste belonging —
A hospital city, sheltering Jews
While men in mechanised armies murdered, bled

On the plains beneath us.' High up there
The afternoon passed, a cloud of Asti Spumante,
Smoke of cigars, and turkey flamed in brandy,
Forming and dissolving into the blue
Of eternal peace . . . . Is it only there
Where vows are real, answers exist to prayer,
And words of love are absolutely true?
The tables emptied as the restaurant cleared

And the groom remembered, 'Yes, I left her there
In the lit compartment, while I took the air
On Foligno platform. They were switching tracks,
Uncoupling carriages off the Ancona train
For the branch to Assisi. Even then, she was free
To go through to Ancona, stay on the plain,
Recover her destiny, never look back,
Or shunt up a siding, live forever with me

In the wrong eternity.' What was she thinking, the bride,
With *Yes*, *Amen* and *Thank You* said,
And the wedding guests avuncular, satisfied,
The fat proprietor waiting to be paid
And stealing crumbs of sweetness off a plate
As Dino and Carlo swabbed the tables clean —
A sacramental wholeness, separating
In sex and religion, sacred and profane,

With the night to come? 'We stood at twelve in the sight
Of good and evil, polychromatic light
Through stained-glass windows, and were joined together —
I, who slept last night through a thunderstorm
While he, in a hotel room, at the end of his tether,
Scared of himself, and sobering up by stages,
Laid out his clothes, and set the alarm
To wake him centuries back, in the Middle Ages.

Believing in permanence.' No one saw them off
Or came to the station. So, they began their life
Unrecognised, in the common waiting-room,
Exploring an ancient jukebox, sharing a beer,
The motherless son, the fatherless daughter,
Wondering when the electric train would come
Up the Tiber valley, into the years,
And the wine of life would turn again to water.

Lachrimae Christi

Christ, if you weep for me,
Bottle your tears, like new Italian wine
I balance between my knees
As the train rolls south from Siena
Through the Apennines

And fruits of intensity
Mellow, the ghostly glide
Of vineyards, vineyards, as we pass them through —
Myself and my bride
Of a week or two.

Purples, yellows —
Salute them! October is here,
And the heartland of Europe, fallow
As an old idea, awaiting its hour
To be found, to recur,

Is brown clay whitening
In the furrows. Trampled juices,
Blood and history, visions of the Nine Muses —
I drank them, like vintage years,
Chianti, or Christ's Tears,

In brothels and oases
Everywhere. Now, for my sins,
Must I take them in, the brown and yellow races,
Exploited girls, and temporary wives,
To trouble our wedded afterlives?

For maybe this is purgatory —
Dante's hills of Tuscany
Riddled with tunnels, electrified
For the passing of twentieth-century trains —
As if I had died

And come back again, to see once more
Conscience, unearthly bride,
Aware, like me, of the chastened countryside,
The ruined homes, from the last World War,
We might have lived inside.

Firenze, Chiusi —
Stations, they speak of limits,
Place in time. The rest is excess.
I see it now, from the afternoon express —
Fidelity to the minute,

Real connections . . . . Christ, divide
The spoils between us — myself and my bride —
A honeymoon couple, balancing bottles of wine
Between our knees, to be drunk at colder temperatures
Further down the line.

Abruzzo

Our days fell into a pattern.
In the mornings, drawing near
With klaxons, grinding gears,
The lorries — climbing
Through thousands of feet
To our mountain village, outside time,
Where we slept on the edge
Of dissolving strata,
Overhangs, frightful gullies —
Awakened us, roared on
With their payload of stone
To the road they would always repeat
Between an abandoned valley
And a future bridge.

It seemed to us, no one else,
Up here, had a job to do —
Least of all ourselves
Around whom the spaces annealed
Like rings of growth, as we ate
Long dinners, me and you,
Alone with our portion of fate,
And hearing, at every hour,
The clack of billiards across in the bar —
Would we join them? The weather
Changed on the peaks, within earshot,
Electric, thundery, hot,
As summer passed, and we cooled our heels
Between one life and another.

White walls, green shutters,
Crusted loaves that smelled of yeast
From the travelling kitchens;
Yellow plums, the fur of peaches
To the hand, ambivalent bells

At funerals and feasts —
All that was tangible, tasted, felt,
Restored us to our senses
Like freezing mountain water
From the spigots, or dialect
Stripped of abstraction, responses
Below language, blurred
And guttural, connecting
Things with their own word.

I said to myself, even then —
Male wholeness, contemplate
The luck you have, with your casual pen,
The luck you may never have again,
Your work, which is also play,
Your house, for which you have not paid,
The new and sacramental light
You see your wife in, maidenly flesh
Accepting you, on the afternoon bed,
Desirable, affectionate,
In short, the miraculous heights
You have raised yourself to, of late —
I wrote it down, one day,
While the knowledge was still fresh.

Watershed

On the spine of Italy
Our train had come to a standstill.

Windows were pulled down
As the temperature rose

And the passengers, heatstruck,
Swatted at clouds of minor irritation.

What was this shadowless station
We were stranded in,

All wind and grasses, the blue whisper
Of alfalfa, growing wild

In a deserted summer
There was no one left to harvest?

They were ours, the abandoned houses,
Ours for the asking,

Like work, or marriage,
Or any ancient principle

Europe forgot, up here in the mountains.
I saw no rivers, starting

In either direction,
No past, no future —

Only a watershed, bearing in
With the weight of the present moment,

Transfiguring us, as we slept
In the shade of our great newspapers

With which we had beaten to death
The gadfly of remembrance.

Firefly

It was zigzagging along
In the dusk, when I snatched it

Out of its path of flight
Like the hand of God

Delaying it, temporarily,
Between the why and the wherefore

Of my cupped palms
That glowed, like a votive lamp

Pulsating yellow, so I knew
It was alive in there

In the attitude of prayer
I carried ahead of me

On the latening road — a principle,
A mustardseed of light

That belonged in the dance of atoms
Around me, energies

The dark released
And I, too, had a hand in.

Taedium Vitae

They came through, the travelling players,
On Sunday, the thirteenth of August,
And the village turned out.

On Monday, a band played in the square,
And the vendors' stalls were soaked
By an electric downpour, the first of autumn.

By Wednesday, it was over. I had been paid
For my casual shifts at the bar
And Roberto gave me back our three children.

When I had cleaned it, the changing-room
We had loaned to the players,
Stale cigarette smoke hung in the air

And I smelled the monotony
Of backstage lives. They had gone with their gear —
And that was it, for another year.

I wish I was back in Trentino again.
I wish there were less winter
Here in the South, in these different mountains

Where no one, not even Roberto,
Sees my slow bleeding
Or the colour draining out of my hair.

Where We Live

Where we live no longer matters
If it ever did, the difference
Between North and East, South and West,
Belfast Central, or Budapest,
Currency changed, like innocence,
For the life that was going to be ours.

Let us admit it. There are powers
No border can contain.
They sit with us, the uninvited guests,
Wherever our table is laid,
Accepting a second coffee,
Awaiting the end of the story.

They were in ourselves
From the beginning. Dark and placeless,
Tropic suns, or the greys of Ulster
Meant nothing to them. Your skies, my skies,
Everywhere in between
Was a place they could work unseen.

Here, they can rest a while
In our latest exile. Groundless,
Taking root anywhere,
Living on thin Italian air,
Our house is their house,
With the bats and the swallows,

Angels and demons, ghosting
The warm red sandstone
Of borrowed quarters. Leave us alone!
Wherever life is an open question
They have beaten us to it
Already, come into their own.

They are the lightnings
That transfigure us, our troubles —
Homeless, the ancient weather
That travels inside us
And breaks out, here or there,
The days we despair of each other.

Meltwater

Somewhere behind all this
I sense the glacier, permanently cold,
We must get back to, at any price,
For the knowledge it withholds
Like a tongue of ice

Translated in green water
Melting . . . . Call it tears
Or semen, a bottle of juniper brandy
Or the distillations of years.
O my wife, whose daughter

Are you — one of the Fates?
Yours is a nameday no one celebrates
In these mountains. Disinherited
Like me, do you love or hate?
Long enough, you have turned into spirit

Juniper berries, straining their seeds
Through meshes of muslin, pickled quinces
For the sweetness they bleed,
And made intensity, measured it out
In fluid ounces.

Long enough, you have cried,
'I remember so little,' into your pillow
And wished you might have died.
Your face was an eddy that tears had blorted,
Ecstasy distorted,

While I swam above you
Looking down, through the waters
Between us, so terrifyingly clear,
That we drink from here —
I, who love you.

Pack your bags. We can start
For the black depressions, drizzling crags
Where the work of the heart
Is accomplished. Miles of tracks
Lead in and back

To what feels like childhood
Already, where to walk is to retrace,
Like babes in the wood,
The steps of avalanche victims
Foetal in ice.

Small Mercies

Affection, the body of a wife,
Ovenlike, stovelike,

Glowing with central warmth
Like a solar plexus,

Succour me, in the dark hours
When the luminous clock

Beats time, and the heart
Is a stationary traveller

Pounding along, directionless.
Great is the riddle

Whose only clue is a pet-name,
And your head, heavy with paradox,

Drowses against me —
I, who have no answers.

Heterae

Towards daybreak, I dreamt again
Of long ago and far away.
A woman, one of the heterae
I had known in a former life,
Was ageing on an endless train.
Asleep beside me, my wife

Kept her own dark rendezvous
With revenants and private ghosts,
Alternatives that rose in hosts
Articulating the unsaid —
Ancestral voices, coming through
From the lives she might have led.

The heterae, the heterae —
I am back again, one autumn day
By a Paris underground station
Awaiting Her, the gorgeous flirt
Who jilts without explanation
Foolish spirits. But no one is hurt.

I wake again, in a barn by the Nore
One winter morning, seeing frost
In spicules on the windowpane,
Ethereal, starlike, galaxies lost
And never to be seen again —
The morning after the night before,

She shifts her body, throws her leg
Companionably over mine,
A Wexford girl, who herds the cattle
Trampling snow outside our door.
Easygoing as Queequeg
She feeds me sexual lore.

I wander the world, and return.
I lose myself, again and again,
Inside a woman, and take the cure,
A restless child, with his fingers burnt
By stolen beauty, stolen fire.
I dream of faces, endless trains.

The heterae, the heterae —
Feckless, inconstant,
Glorying in the instant,
Are they angels or demons?
What is the knowledge I betrayed
In choosing to be human?

Awake beside my wife, I lay.
In a minute, or an hour,
When the common light of day
Had turned her inside out again,
I would see the dark power
In her eyes, and the other men.

In Hoc Signo

The straws in the wind —
Who feeds on them? Nobody here
Is poor enough,

Thank God. The starving cats
And mongrels have the rubbish bin
And the poor in spirit

Seek solace in the bar.
The door of the church is always locked
Since the chalice was stolen,

But the heraldic animals
Stabled for winter
Are safe as in Ark or Manger.

Christmas approaches.
Blue Adriatic mists
Creep inland, up our valley —

The winds from Greece
Reversing themselves, occluding us
At the desired height

Of contemplation.
Plato and the Gospels,
She and I — what more do we need

Than our two bodies, our two minds,
To link each other
And the world we left behind?

Sometimes, out of the blue,
A telephone rings, rings off —
The outer world trying to get through,

The buzz and static
Of interconnected voices —
Europe, America . . .

Then nothing. Silence.
A horsebell in the mists,
Time dripping from the eaves,

The IN HOC SIGNO of the bar,
The closed church —
And a cripple, playing Patience

Under dirty yellow streetlights,
Greeting us in the English
He learned as a prisoner of war.

At the Grave of Silone

Lost in the fog at four thousand feet
When the lights come on, I can see them all,
The mountain villages, so small
A blind man feels his way about
Without a stick, and everyone overhears
Everyone else, as they quarrel and shout,
And still they are all alone —
And the places, the years,
Who redeems them? I think again
Of you, Ignazio Silone,
Ten years dead, a hundred miles to the south
On this freezing Apennine chain,
A body interred, forever looking out
On an endlessly fertile plain —

And how we had visited you, one day
When August blew the crops awake
And harvesters toiled, in the drained lake
Of human promise . . . . Skies were passing away
But nothing had changed on the ground.
Heat and apathy, everyday sound
In your natal village. Unsuccess
With its local dreamers, revving their motorbikes,
Punishing the slot machines.
Fontamara . . . it could have been
Aranyaprathet, or Ballaghaderreen.
Without knowing it, we had come to pray
At the shrine of ordinariness —
We, who were running away.

And look at us now, a man and woman
Dodging the Reaper, saving hay
In the high Abruzzo, our windowpanes
Rattled by cold, and the sonic vibrations,
Extraterrestrial, superhuman,

Of half a dozen airforce planes
That shatter the peace . . . . Again, night falls
On this village of limitations
We have come to. Invisible forces spray
Their DUCE-VINCEREMO on our walls.
As your books say,
All of us dream, and stay in thrall
To the usual consolations.
Marriage. America. Going away.

I shut the window, bank the fire,
And pick up Plato on The Good.
The lumberjack, who gives us wood
For nothing, I see him across in the bar
Where a girl is slicing lemons, tidying shelves,
And shadows argue, the porkpie hats
Of failures home from Canada, playing skat
And fourhand poker. Metal crutches,
Phlegm — the man absurdity trails
Like a village dog . . . If they saw themselves
For just one instant, as they are,
Heroic, but misunderstood,
Their conversations would carry for miles
Like the sound of a shot.

Castelli, Cerqueto, cold San Giorgio
Float in the fog, red atmospheres
Connected to each other, and to here,
Where I link your fate with hers and mine,
Unconsciousness everywhere . . . . Fifty years ago,
In exile, writing *Bread and Wine*,
The War was coming. Now, below your shrine,
Memory tries to wake
Blind monuments to the Fascist dead,
Disheartened villages, men who cannot shake

The ant of toil from their Sunday clothes,
Slatternly women, old for their years,
The Christian cross, the Communist rose,
With the human word you said.

The River

When I was angry, I went to the river —
New water on old stones, the patience of pools.
Let the will find its own pace,
Said a voice inside me
I was learning to believe,

And the rest will take care of itself.
The fish were facing upstream, tiny trout
Suspended like souls, in their aquaeous element.
I and my godlike shadow
Fell across them, and they disappeared.

All this happened deep in the mountains —
Anger, trout, and shadow
With the river flowing through them.
Far away, invisible but imagined,
Was an ancient sea, where things would resolve themselves.

To the Orsini Family

If a phrase floats into my mind
Suggestive of these heights, I will owe it to you,
Ancestral patrons, who made life hell
For the thief on the gibbet, the ancient ringer of bells
In this village where I write.
It was you controlled the passes
On every mountain, who waited for snow and sleet
To deliver to your mercies
Robber bands, abroad without inheritance
In the Abruzzo wastes,
And brought the wolf to your streets.

Plenipotentiaries, lords of life and death,
Exacting from your peasantry
Taxes in salt, for a temporal pope
Whose crucifix gathers dust at the back of the vestry,
I see the decline of your castle keep
To a ruined cellar, centuries deep
Beneath the hard clang of a bell without resonance
On a Sunday afternoon. The soul is asleep
In a dull contentment, everyone's needs have been met.
In your fifteenth-century watchtower
A priest is dying yet.

If this is called moderation
Thank you, Signori. The knock of bowls against wood,
Demotic speech of cardplayers
In the old men's tavern, and this gentle art
I practise, at the back end of Europe,
In a lost mountain dialect —
Lyric poetry. All your wars have been fought
And taciturnity reigns
In the defeated. Far below me, the plains

Administer in the name of enlightenment,
And it is to them I look, in lieu of genius,
For the power of consecutive thought.

In Earthquake Country

Slow as a landscape, character forms
In front of us, through a window in the mountains
Looking inwards and outwards together
At lines of nature, sandstone weathering,
Rifts that open between us, rifts that dissolve,
Except for the seams in our faces
As we grow older.

Look north, at the Apennines,
Their old faultlines. Earthquake country —
Blind tectonic plates
Are shifting the ground beneath us,
Our mediterranean floor. Forget villages
And forests of dwarf oak. Here, life
Roots itself in the inhuman.

A valley of soulmaking —
Where does it lead to? Glacial waters meet
Down there, where we cannot see them,
Roaring in our ears
All night, while we hold each other
In this cold planetarium of lights
That closes us in, the children of Galileo.

Do they see us, as we see ourselves,
The windows turning gold? Good night, dear heart,
And better luck than the dead
From Naples to Avezzano — histories, loves
Before our time, that the epicentres swallowed —
While faith that moves mountains
Tolls upvalley, in its fissured belltower.

Crossing the Apennines

In Spring, we went back to the high valleys,
You and I. Already, there were cyclamens
Huddled together for warmth, like the flames of a primus stove
On the cold forest floor. Empty woods
Awaiting leafage, drenched in April light,
A roar of mountain water
Everywhere in earshot. Electric,
Inquisitive, animals puzzled us out
For the strangers we were, with the Roman road beneath us
Cut like a groove of ageless repetition
Out of the winter. Healing mosses,
Moist green sphagnum, thickened
Like patches of living warmth, on the north face of everything.

There was always another side, but we lived on this side,
So close beneath our own particular mountain
We lost sight of it. Even now,
With the visibility clearing
On the high arêtes, there was something brooding
Out of doors, that had cooped us in seclusion
Months on end, stalled
In a wintry kitchen, icepicks hung on the wall,
A hearth of cold ashes, and trouble gathering head
In our darker selves . . . .
                              I would like to say
We crossed the Apennines, kept to the ancient way
As so many had done before us —
Watersheds, the invisible line
Where intuition is strengthened
And love becomes certainty. No, it was not like that.
Leached soils, yes, and the bones of cattle
At six thousand feet, where the snowline started.
And those impossibly high meadows
Where silent horses surrounded us, like trusting spirits
Expecting sugar, and we fed them salt.

Taking the Waters

There are taps that flow, all day and all night,
From the depths of Europe,
Inexhaustible, taken for granted,

Slaking our casual thirsts
At a railway station
Heading south, or here in the Abruzzo

Bursting cold from an iron standpipe
While our blind mouths
Suck at essentials, straight from the water table.

Our health is too good, we are not pilgrims,
And the nineteenth century
Led to disaster. Aix, and Baden Baden —

Where are they now, those ladies with the vapours
Sipping at glasses of hydrogen sulphide
Every morning, while the pumphouse piano played

And Russian radicals steamed and stewed
For hours in their sulphur tubs
Plugged in to the cathodes of Revolution?

Real cures, for imaginary ailments —
Diocletian's, or Vespasian's.
History passes, only the waters remain,

Bubbling up, through their carbon sheets,
To the other side of catastrophe
Where we drink, at a forgotten source,

Through the old crust of Europe
Centuries deep, restored by a local merchant
Of poultry and greens, inscribing his name in Latin.

PART TWO

The Fish Laboratory

In the afterlife, our footfalls
Will be soundless, and the fish
Will go on feeding
Undisturbed, in their breeding ponds
At the bottom of our minds —
And the weather will always be early winter
Like today, the sun cold
On the blue of Lake Trasimeno,
Time at a standstill.

Go quietly. As it is,
We cast long shadows
And the earth vibrates
With dark, invisible tremors —
Our feet in passing . . . . Instincts
Bunch and flee, afraid of the light
In their green translucent tanks
And floating cages. Broodfish
Wintering, time in suspension,
And ourselves, dear heart,
On the wooden footbridge.

There are stopcocks, temperature gauges.
A warm spermatic odour
From the fishmeal bins, pervading
Nose and throat. Oxygenated,
The water pulses, like a heartbeat,
Through the startled ponds. November —
And the cycle of creation
Is complete. The fifth season
Reeks of fishes. Disengaged
Among breeding strains and variants,
Genetic lines, the man
In the white laboratory coat
Would wash his hands, now, like God the Father.

'If you return,' he says, 'in the early Spring,
When the waters are green again
With a frenzy of multiplication,
And pike, their spawning imminent,
Turn on each other, and bite
In brute appetite, wallow and thrash —
You will see us at work, who strip
The underbelly of time
In Kannegeiter glasses, whirligigs,
Centrifugal, for the dervish dance
Of sperm and egg . . . . '
                              The nets for the soul
Are lifted, and the afterlife
Spreads like Lake Trasimeno,
Blue, serene, in the early winter
Empty of bird migrations. Far to the south
The white storks gather, instincts of generation
On their wintering grounds —
But this is where I locate us
Out of season, before and after
The baptism by immersion
In the dark water of our lives.

The Better Portion

The husband loved early mornings.
But the wife, give or take
The twenty percent in all of us
Open to change, slept on
To a different clock, her nightgown
A rectangle of white calico
Cut from the template of darkness.

Light changed in the various rooms
But only he saw it . . . . Afternoons
Were their common ground — the hot infusions
Brewed at four, the casual chat
As something came to the boil
Or simmered away, depending
On who was in charge, and who not,

And which year it was. Outside
Could have been anywhere, a world
Improvised, for argument's sake,
From the barking of neighbourhood dogs
Or a car backfiring, smells
And habits, the usual bottomless wells —
But this is beside the point,

As all who are paid to listen
Could have told him . . . .
                              Suddenly
One evening, she talked a blue streak
From half-past-eleven
To four-fifteen, then fell asleep
Like a stone disappearing into the deep.
All this comes from nowhere,

He told himself, flabbergasted
And unmanned, with the working surface
Of marriage all around him
To hold on to — heart and head,
The better portion neither disputed
In all their years of breaking bread
Before she emerged, from the underworld.

The Poet Sandro Penna, in Old Age

There are those who will leave this world
On a gun-carriage, draped in the flag of the state
Like my friend Montale,
Always so careful, always so astute,
So politically in the right,
With his place in the Senate, his Nobel prize
Like a state of grace
This side, at least, of eternal night —

And there are those, like my old friend
Pasolini, his bloodied head
Kicked in by a male prostitute
In Ostia — it could so easily
Have been him and me! —
Splashed all over the Roman evening papers,
Coming, in public, to scandalous ends
In the underworld of the id —

And there is me,
Sandro Penna, turned seventy
Last summer, without votes of congratulation
Or unexpurgated editions
Of the sexual poems. A fancier of boys
All my life, I have been.
For this the critics call me 'The last of the Greeks,
The most ancient of men . . . . '

Ernesto, Quintilio, beloved Raffaele —
A cigarette or an ice-cream
Could buy your caresses, outside the Termini Station.
To the conviction of your beauty I held fast
When the tortured screams

From Gestapo headquarters rang in our ears
Through the endless months of the German occupation.
Did you only recognise me
By my bitten nails, like all pederasts?*

Nembutal, Mogadon, Tavar, and Mictasol
Turning my urine blue —
I am old, alone. My reputation? It's invisible —
A poet, they say, for the very few
Who see, through the mists of the twentieth century,
The universal, the sun coming through.
To the journalists
I can only say, not even trying to make sense,
'My past is risible . . . . '

---

*Roman street lore, 1930s.

Travel

Knowing nothing, I went to Ephesus
Two thousand years too late

For Mary in mourning, Greek debate,
The closure of the Milesian schools.

What I had not learned already
I never would. That God is love

And everything else is water,
Thales himself, or one of his Turkish daughters,

The dark, fatebearing women
I always have been drawn to

Could have told me, as I washed
Unsuccessfully, in the mud of the marketplace —

A standing joke, for thousands of years,
To Heraclitus and his peers.

But no one told me. For all I knew
A million Christs had been and gone

Through Ephesus, the relative zone,
Its ruins crying to the Absent One,

And I could go back home
Like Pythagoras, to my own dear land,

And carry on staring at heaven
And tracing lines in sand.

Letter from the South

The dead heat, the white haze
Of mindlessness, spreading
Inertia through the dogdays

Puts me to bed here, stalled,
Regressive, through the long afternoons.
My bloodshot yellow walls

Are all I know of light.
The shutters are down
All over Italy — empty towns

The Africans drift into,
Blown Sahara dust
On our jaundiced windows,

A wild whisper, trapped in the eaves,
Sirocco . . . .
                    Out of boredom
Are the children conceived

Who repopulate these deserts
Barren of reason?
The body alone is in season

Always and forever,
Obedient to earth's laws.
We are too cold, too clever —

But who else can I talk to
Since you have gone?
The mind is asleep, the body withdrawn,

The whole of life in suspension.
Come back to me, remember
Intellect, books, the fertile tension . . . .

Wake me in September
When my head clears
And I look again at the years

We have still together.
Loveless necessity, parched blue weather
And the cold water of gossip

Possess everyone. Word of mouth
Has it we are separate.
This is the news from the far south.

Eclogue

Umbrian headspace, let me in on you
This once, like a secret
That is the same secret everywhere.
Stripped of your placenames — Spello, Assisi —
What are you, but subjectivity
Sweating, in the roots of my own hair,

As I fiddle to break new ground
On a sheet of paper? Disclose yourself
While I still have an hour to spare
And the shadowless squares
Are deserted. Grant me the grace
Of a new condition of mind,

The mind of Umbria, for instance,
Saturated in hot light,
Its priests and middlemen driven indoors,
Its churches all gone quiet
After centuries, in a noontide
Of the soul, a lucid despair

That is older than any religion.
The blue deepens, the crops swelter
Under fantails of water
From the sprinklers. Aftersmells
Of mown hay cling to the nostrils.
Obsolete heavens, obsolete hells

Are frescoes on abandoned walls.
Layers of perception
Peel and hang — the Virgin Birth,
The Casting Out of Devils
In Montefalco, Good and Evil.
But now is the hour of an actual earth

Insisting forever 'Climb down
Off the plane of ideality
And look again, at the desolate town
Of Santa Maria degli Angeli,
Where the girls are women
At fourteen, mothers at twenty,

Done in, broken-chested,
The ghost of an early perfection
In their faces — and the boys
Hot-rodding, on speed and noise,
Whizzing into futurity
On a whiff of benzine, spiritual exhaust.'

Half-past-twelve, in the windless region.
Crook-crook go the bluegrey pigeons
Under my eaves. Anaesthetised,
Drenched in ammonia, the land drowses
In fertile tracts, out of Virgil.
Off the shuttered houses

Lightwaves bounce. Not a breeze
Anywhere. They will go to bed,
Those two, she will bring him to a head . . . .
And the mercury static, at thirty degrees,
As I tap the glass
Abstractedly, and the mood passes.

The Walled Town

If I lived where there were still wolves,
Or the myth of wolves, my town would have walls,
My neighbours, instructing themselves
On fresco cycles, like televised government,
Would never read or write at all,

Too human for politics, just as we are today,
When a Nordic motorcyclist, the first one for ages,
Fills the square with his terrible horsepower,
And seems, by his very attitude, to enquire,
'Did Frederic Barbarossa come this way?
And how could his army, collective as fate,
Pass through so tiny a gate?'

He looks and he listens. Dirty linen, and catcalls.
A pretty divorcée in a miniskirt
Who deals in antiques, and raises a child on her own.
And footballs, the thud of footballs
On the inside walls of limit, of the known.

What does he see in us? Something innate
Like his own lost childhood? Could he live among us
Praying to a cardiac muscle on a plate,
Our sanctified relic? Or is it our view of the plains
He wants to commandeer, for his next campaign?
Could he satisfy, if he took our women as wives,
His hunger for integral life?

Dostoyevsky to his Publisher Stellovsky, Florence 1869

for Peter Fallon

'Today it rained, and I thought again of home.
It was one of those rare days, when the wind
Shifts quarter, and brews up a storm
On the Apennines. If I looked from my window,
The blue smoke of a thousand chimneypots,
Blowing southward, was all I could see. And it pleased me!
It pleased me, the drenched and windblown carriages
Of artlovers, drawn up in front of the Pitti —
I already know the masterpieces by heart —
And damp on yellow houses, the wet cobblestones
Of empty squares, the public driven indoors —
Let them suffer like us! Let them learn what it is to be grey!

So I drank tea, while smells of cooking wafted
From the families below, their quarrels and violent sneezing
And everything shouted out at the tops of their voices,
Unselfconscious as children, and as innocent —
Reading the Russian papers, three days late,
The terrorist trials, Nechayev *versus* The State,
Wanting to smell again that desolate air
Of the motherland, without which imagination dies
And conscience atrophies. Here, they do not understand me,
They to whom beauty is handed on a plate,
The Fiorentini. They are too goodnatured
As it is. Our world means nothing to them . . . .

Anna Snitkina is pregnant again —
We will move north to Dresden, to the German midwives
That much nearer home. If there were even vice
To daemonise me! But the gambling halls
Are shut by order of law. A year or two yet
And even our literary enemies — and our debts —

Will seem like Holy Russia, as we cross
The frontier, in a third-class train,
Exile behind us, the convict's ball and chain
Of inescapable suffering to come home to
Like maturity, or the predestined way,
And turn our backs on Europe, once and for all.'

The Nihilists

First they were only noise in the next room
And chaos approaching. Then, they were admitted —
Acquaintances, you might say, of the third degree
And the lower depths, though swallowtailed, tophatted,
Much as we were ourselves. 'I disagree!'
They were already shouting, even among each other,
'A hundred million heads? Too high a price
To bring about, on the corpses of our fathers,
The certainty of an earthly paradise?'
I sat them down as usual, ordered tea,
And let the eternal argument resume

I first had heard in Eighteen Sixty Seven.
Old nobility, flirting with the New
In Petersburg, so many years ago,
I shuddered to remember monies given
Into the secret coffers of God knows who.
Then, I was undecided. Now, I knew.
The best I could hope for was to clear my throat
And get a word in edgeways, waste a quote
On these poor *raznochinetsi* — sneers, contempt —
In French or German, Voltaire, Diderot,
The laughable ghosts of the Enlightenment

They had done away with. 'Did you know,'
A girl began deliberately, as she pared
Her fingernails, in the best modern manner,
Onto my drawingroom carpet, looked me through —
Her insolent blue spectacles, cropped hair —
'Mrs Terentyev has taken a lover —
No, I should not say lover, but a friend —
And left her husband, dead of a broken heart.
Together with Miss Varetz, they will go
In the name of rational happiness, to start
A commune in the Petersburg East End.'

Another sat at the piano, vamped a waltz
To keep the streets in ignorance outside.
I realised a thousand years had died
While I, and people like me everywhere,
Pretended interest in the Social Question,
Toured our estates, exchanged hot air
On cholera, cattle plague, and good digestion,
Brought our ladies round with smelling salts
To face domestic boredom, puerperal fever,
Childbirth or miscarriage, once a year,
A nineteenth-century waltz going on forever . . . .

Yes, we were guilty. Vast allodial lands
And forests that we never should have sold,
And families of serfs we lost at cards,
Our faked returns, our traffic in dead souls —
In Switzerland, Siberia, they planned
And theorised on Ireland, Italy —
Backward, too, but advanced in misery —
And never doubted that the day would come
To return from exile, at a word
Unleash millenial forces, put to flame
Countries of wooden houses, all the same.

'Give us the money for a printing press
And we'll let you be — ' Who put them up to it?
A divinity student in tarred peasant boots
Slurped from his saucer. Trembling like a leaf
A boy consumptive — feverish, glittering eyes —
Crepitated blood in his handkerchief.
I asked myself again: If this is youth . . .
Another hundred years would have to pass
While they construed, from my noncommittal smile,
Rearguard wars, and massacres. Meanwhile,
The lie I lived was better than the truth.

Søren Kierkegaard

I took you north with me, Kierkegaard,
Always intending to read you. On the train
I had nine straight hours, from Florence through to Munich
In a closed compartment . . . . Marshalling yards
At Bologna, the north Italian plain

That seemed to stretch forever — apples, wine,
The childhood of humanity, acres of vines
And orchards blossoming with original sin
Through windows looking outwards, looking in.
I never got down to it, your grand design —

The Stages on Life's Way were watersheds
I stretched my legs at, took the air
At fabulous, but earthly, altitudes,
Where Austrians boarded, girls with golden hair.
Serious, bookish, riding the corridors

Into Germany, scions of adult races,
These are your readership, Kierkegaard.
The ethical life, the Protestant rage
At ecstasy, bought at a station —
I never got beyond the opening page.

Kierkegaard, I can see you shake your head
In disappointment at the sons of men
From everywhere north of the Alps, a land of the dead
Your spirit inhabits, ghosting your own books —
The Sickness Unto Death. The Concept of Dread.

Bavarian traffic streams through the needle's eye
Of a manmade tunnel. Almost done
Our northward journey, and the autobahn
Keeps pace with us, converging
On Munich . . . . What would you know of joy,

Kierkegaard, you who hated poets,
Or the million things that pass through one man's mind
In nine hours' transit, all the way through from Florence,
Feeding his soul on headphones,
Dreaming of women. Things you would not understand.

Dachau, April 1990

Beyond Obermenzig, the countryside begins
At Allach, Karlsfeld, all the way to Dachau,
But there are still smokestacks, the fumes
Of productivity, steep-roofed suburbs
Off which the snow slides easily — yesterday's snow,
Like memory . . . .
                            So it is no surprise
To stand in this bare white space, and feel nothing,
And know that beyond the sizzle of high voltage
There is only nature, coming into season
Like something lobotomised, at peace with itself
In a mindless contentment. Upper Bavaria,
Sweet are your pastures, soft as a woman's breast,
As undulant, rolling. I could lay my head this minute
In your flowering grasses, and go to sleep forever.
There was a bad dream once, but now it is over.

Sing me to sleep. Let others, for my sake,
The bared and shaven heads of *Häftlinge*
Twenty-four hours at attention, stay awake
In the consciousness of evil. Century's end —
And the gates are closing behind us, letting us out
To whom the future belongs . . . .
                            I remember nothing —
And it is so comfortable now, the smooth transitions
On the electric train, through to the centre of Munich
In twenty minutes. So late in the century
The tired mind yawns, the crowds are rushing home,
Emotionless, from whatever their work has been,
And no one sees himself, on the telescreens
Hung like conscience, in the public places,
Blind spots blown up huge, like anamnesis
Or the bare white space where memory should be.

The Skull of Martin Bormann

And who, you may ask,
Is Martin Bormann, that his skull
Should take to task

The blondes astride the Berlin Wall
As the City of Man grows whole again
And the powers fall?

A shade on an underground train.
A handful of radioactive dust
Whose trace is lost

Somewhere between Weidendammer Brücke
And the hell of the Lehrter Station.
If it wanted to, it could not speak

For the din of generations
Drunk on freedom, drowning the past
In a sea of pink carnations —

'I, whose name is legion,
Dreamt, like you, of the bourgeois life.
Crowd-fever, contagion

Of history, storm and strife
Resolved, at last, in the perfect nation.
My nothingness, or call it tact,

Stood behind every dictator —
Phantom husband, phantom wife —
Whose marriage was a suicide pact,

And ended up in No Man's Land,
Adolf Hitler my only friend,
Everyone else a traitor.'

Night Train through the Brenner

Why should it seem so strange
To be travelling backwards
Out of Germany, as the hours change,

With the whole of history
In reverse, the passengers sleeping
On fettered wheels, and everyone in the dark?

When we left, it was after midnight.
New Year rockets fizzling out
On the Munich streets — a litter of celebration,

Firecrackers, broken glass,
And two hundred years of revolution
Lingering, like a sulphur smell in the nostrils . . . .

The conductor coughs in the corridor
All night long. He can have our identities
If he gives them back in the morning

Rubberstamped. Our one desire
Is to sleep in the peace
Of body heat — let no torch shine among us! —

While someone else deciphers
The moving lights from their reflections,
The true direction of time . . . .

The Alps are not our business —
Innsbrück, Brenner, Bolzano. A roar in our ears
As we bore through tunnels —

The watersheds of Europe
Were always too cold for us. Better to dream
Of Munich with its Christmas lights

Or the mannequins of Florence,
At one of which we will certainly wake
The morning after the ages.

Towards daybreak, the sound of voices —
An unknown station. How long have we been here?
An hour? A night? Two hundred years?

Italian speech, on a megaphone
' . . . *Bologna, Firenze, binario tre* . . . '
Drifts through the darkness. Been and gone

Is Nineteen Hundred and Eighty Nine —
The heights are behind us. Early vendors
Push their steaming trolleys

Through the small hours of Day One.
Two tramps, a railwayman,
In the light of a station buffet,

Swallow their bitter portion. For an instant
Life is the same for all of us,
Bleary-eyed, at the dawn of humanity.

The Canto of Ulysses

As the eye reads, from left to right,
Ulysses' canto, what comes next,
The day, already spread like a text
On the ceiling above me, asks to be read.
Anxiety, or increasing light,
Whatever wakes me, fills my head
With the oceanic billows
Of a slept-in marriage bed.

The shutters go up, like thunder,
On the street below. If the soul fed
On coffee, aromatic bread,
Niceties raised to the power of art,
We would long ago have knuckled under
To perfection, in the green heart
Of Italy, settled here,
And gone to sleep in the years.

But what was it Dante said
About ordinary life? My mind wanders
Like Ulysses, through the early sounds,
A motor starting, taps turned on,
Unravelling Penelope's skein,
Unsatisfied, for the millionth time,
With merely keeping my feet on the ground —
As if I could ever go home!

Money, like a terrible shadow,
Unsuccess, and middle age,
Darken my vision of the page
I scan from memory, where it says
Women will all be widows
To the quest, neglected fathers,
Ageing, live out lonely days,
And coastlines merge with each other.

Sound of a passing train at dawn
Through Umbrian fields, of wheat and vines,
Through cloisters and bird sanctuaries,
Feeding on overhead powerlines,
Obsesses me, like the need to be gone,
Vitality, or cowardice,
The sail of Ulysses, west of the sun,
Dwindling in ptolemaic skies.

What did you say to me last night?
'Where you go, I go.' Sleep on that
While I watch you, curled,
Uxorious, my one satisfaction
At the heart of the known world,
Stippled with mediterranean light,
Its yellow streaks already latent
With afternoon heat, and stupefaction.

Any day now, we hand back the key
To habit, peace, stability,
The seasonal round, festivities
Of wine and cherry. Think of the fuss
Of what to take, and leave behind —
Shade for the soul, our miniature trees
Of olive, oak, and southern pine —
Before the seas close over us.